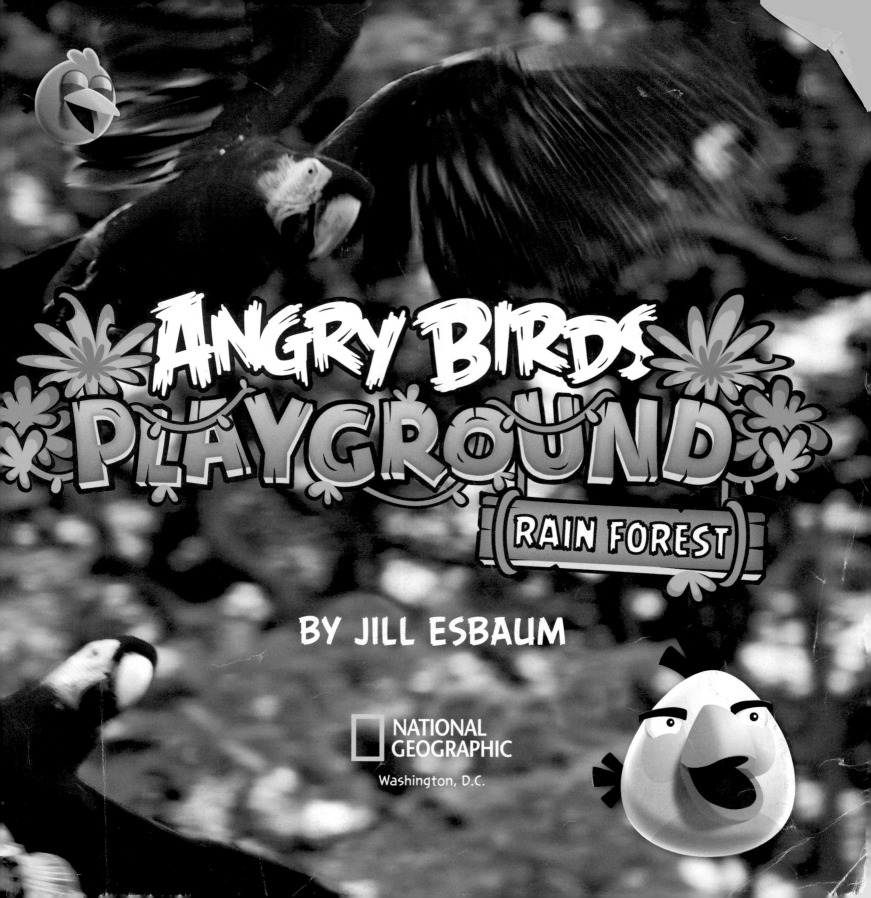

# ANGRY BIRDS
# PLAYGROUND
## RAIN FOREST

BY JILL ESBAUM

NATIONAL
GEOGRAPHIC

Washington, D.C.

For Calvin

The National Geographic Society is one of the world's largest nonprofit scientific and educational organizations. Founded in 1888 to "increase and diffuse geographic knowledge," the Society's mission is to inspire people to care about the planet. It reaches more than 400 million people worldwide each month through its official journal, National Geographic, and other magazines; National Geographic Channel; television documentaries; music; radio; films; books; DVDs; maps; exhibitions; live events; school publishing programs; interactive media; and merchandise. National Geographic has funded more than 10,000 scientific research, conservation and exploration projects and supports an education program promoting geographic literacy.

For more information, please visit nationalgeographic.com, call 1-800-NGS LINE (647-5463), or write to the following address:
National Geographic Society
1145 17th Street N.W.
Washington, D.C. 20036-4688 U.S.A.

Visit us online at **nationalgeographic.com/books**
For librarians and teachers: **ngchildrensbooks.org**
More for kids from National Geographic: **kids.nationalgeographic.com**
For information about special discounts for bulk purchases, please contact National Geographic Books Special Sales: **ngspecsales@ngs.org**
For rights or permissions inquiries, please contact National Geographic Books Subsidiary Rights: **ngbookrights@ngs.org**

Hardcover ISBN: 978-1-4263-1685-2
Library Edition ISBN: 978-1-4263-1688-3

Printed in the United States of America
14/CK-CML/1

# Contents

# MAP OF THE AMAZON

The Amazon rain forest, covering much of South America, is the largest rain forest in the world. It is often called the lungs of the planet. That's because its millions of trees and plants take carbon dioxide gas out of the air and put back oxygen that people and animals need to breathe. The rain forest puts so much moisture and oxygen into the air that it affects weather around the world.

The rain forest is also home to millions of animals and plants. Some live in the waters of the mighty Amazon River that flows through the region. Many others live and grow in the forest itself. Scientists divide the forest into layers: the forest floor, the understory, the canopy, and the emergent. Each layer is perfect for the types of animals that live there.

OUR RAIN FOREST ADVENTURE BEGINS WITH A VISIT TO THE AMAZON RIVER TO MEET A FEW OF THE ANIMALS THAT LIVE IN THIS WATERY HOME.

PACIFIC OCEAN

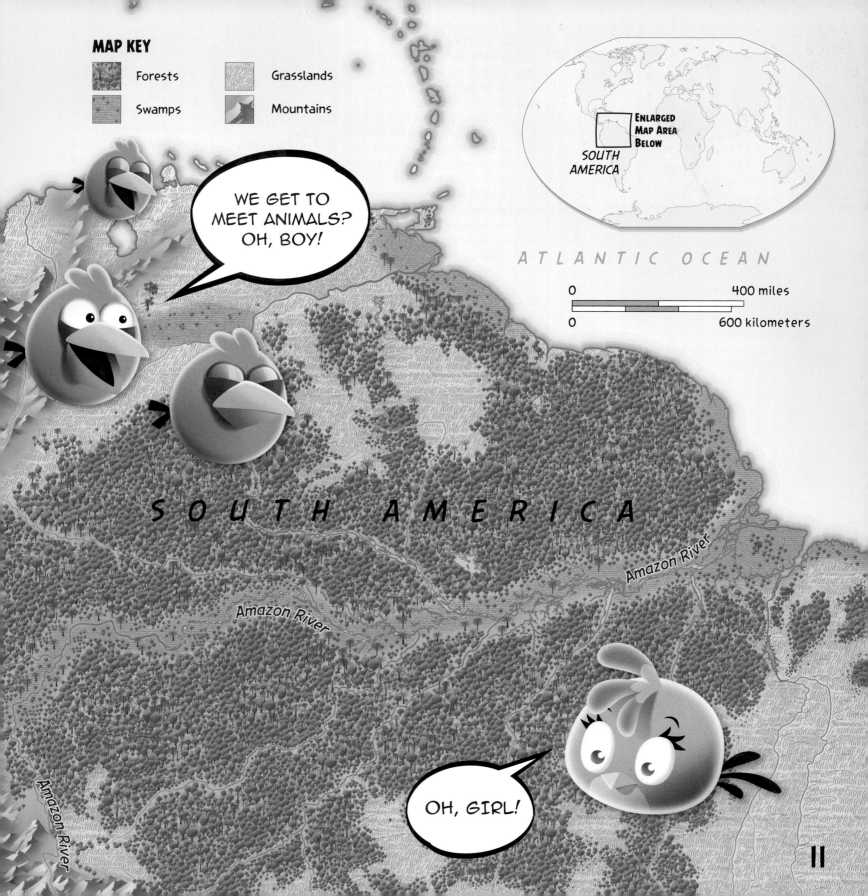

# THE FOREST LAYERS

The rain forest has five different layers where plants and animals live.

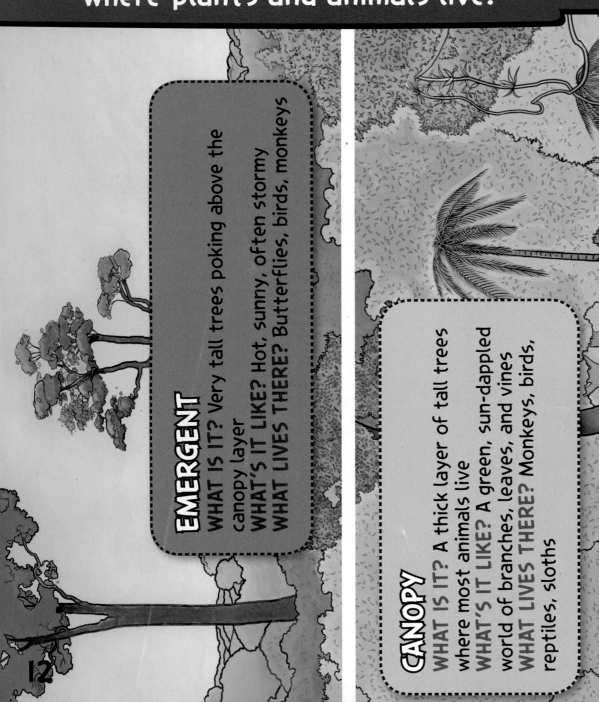

## EMERGENT
WHAT IS IT? Very tall trees poking above the canopy layer
WHAT'S IT LIKE? Hot, sunny, often stormy
WHAT LIVES THERE? Butterflies, birds, monkeys

## CANOPY
WHAT IS IT? A thick layer of tall trees where most animals live
WHAT'S IT LIKE? A green, sun-dappled world of branches, leaves, and vines
WHAT LIVES THERE? Monkeys, birds, reptiles, sloths

## UNDERSTORY
WHAT IS IT? Short, wide-leaved trees
WHAT'S IT LIKE? Dark, tangled
WHAT LIVES THERE? Tree frogs, insects, jaguars

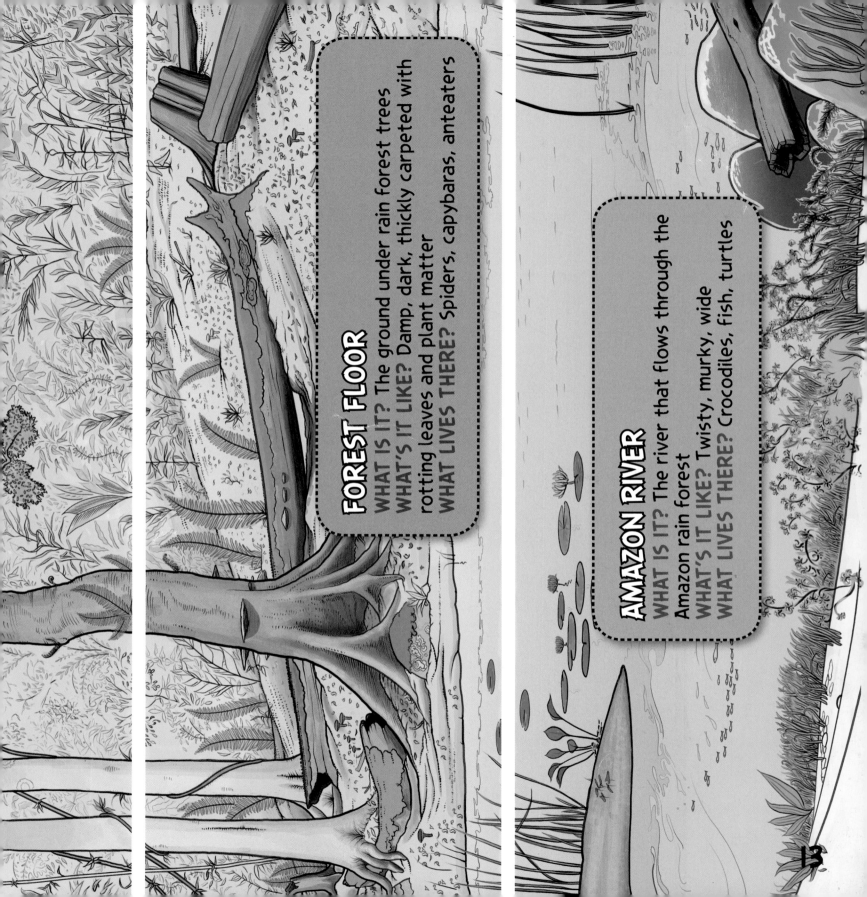

## FOREST FLOOR

**WHAT IS IT?** The ground under rain forest trees
**WHAT'S IT LIKE?** Damp, dark, thickly carpeted with rotting leaves and plant matter
**WHAT LIVES THERE?** Spiders, capybaras, anteaters

## AMAZON RIVER

**WHAT IS IT?** The river that flows through the Amazon rain forest
**WHAT'S IT LIKE?** Twisty, murky, wide
**WHAT LIVES THERE?** Crocodiles, fish, turtles

# TO THE AMAZON RIVER BASIN!

The Amazon rain forest is in a part of South America called the Amazon River Basin. "Basin" is just a word for a large area of land with a river flowing through it. All of the smaller rivers and streams in that basin flow into one big river—the Amazon.

The Amazon River Basin is huge—about the same size as the United States (minus Alaska and Hawaii). Within this vast basin are areas of dry grassland, lakes and swamps, and the largest rain forest in the world. Winding and twisting through the middle of it all is the wide Amazon River.

14

15

# LOOKING AT THE LAYERS:
# THE RIVER BASIN

## RIVER BASIN

More than 200 rivers and streams flow into the Amazon River.

UNDISCOVERED ANIMALS? MAYBE THEY'RE INVISIBLE.

Thousands of different kinds of animals live in the Amazon River, many still undiscovered by humans!

OR REALLY GOOD AT HIDE-AND-SEEK!

The Amazon River is the world's second longest (after Africa's Nile River). It is 4,000 miles (6,437 km) long. No bridge crosses it.

The Amazon River is from one to six miles (1.6 to 10 km) wide during the dry season. During the rainy season, the river floods and becomes many miles wider.

PRETTY! TOO BAD THEY DON'T HAVE FEATHERS.

These dolphins may look like ocean dolphins, but they are only distantly related. The Amazon river dolphin, called boto in Brazil, needs fresh water to survive, not salt water. Some are bubble gum pink, but others might be pale pink—or even off-white or blue-gray or tan.

Their long snouts are excellent for poking among tree roots or prodding a muddy river bottom in search of a meal.

A river dolphin's back teeth are wide and flat, better for chewing and grinding (like ours!).

SIZE: **LENGTH:** UP TO 9 FEET (2.7 M) **WEIGHT:** UP TO 300 POUNDS (136 KG)

**ON THE MENU:** FISH, TURTLES

**FUN FACT:** THE SUN CAN FADE THESE DOLPHINS. LIVING IN MUDDY WATER HELPS THEM STAY PINK.

# ELECTRIC EEL

RIVER BASIN

This beast looks a little dangerous. And it is. An electric eel can put out an electric shock powerful enough to knock down a horse. Less powerful zaps are used for hunting—to stun fish—as well as to discourage predators.

Electric eels breathe air, so they need to surface from time to time and take a gulp. They aren't really eels, actually, but fish. They are more closely related to catfish than to the eels that live in Earth's oceans.

**SIZE: LENGTH:** UP TO 8 FEET (2.5 M) **WEIGHT:** UP TO 44 POUNDS (20 KG)

**ON THE MENU:** INVERTEBRATES LIKE CRAB AND SHRIMP, FISH, AND SMALL MAMMALS

**FUN FACT:** ELECTRIC EELS CANNOT SEE VERY WELL, SO THEY SEND OUT VERY SMALL ELECTRICAL BLIPS THAT BOUNCE OFF OBJECTS AND BACK TO THE EEL. THIS HELPS IT FIND ITS WAY AROUND AND LOCATE PREY.

ELECTRIC ZAPPERS! LET'S TAKE ONE HOME.

# GIANT RIVER OTTER

RIVER BASIN

I LIKE THESE GUYS.

22

Otters are playful, fun-loving animals...but they'll fight to the death to protect their families. Family groups live in dens burrowed into the banks of slow-moving rivers or creeks.

These otters all have white patches on their throats, but no two patches are exactly alike. They have thick fur, webbed feet, and powerful tails that make them excellent swimmers. When these mammals need to go underwater, their ears and nostrils close to keep water out.

Once hunted for its fur, the giant river otter is now one of the rarest otters in the world.

YEAH, THEY PROTECT THEIR FAMILIES.

LIKE WE PROTECT OUR EGGS!

SIZE: **LENGTH:** UP TO 6 FEET (1.8 M)
**WEIGHT:** 75 POUNDS (34 KG)

**ON THE MENU:** FISH AND CRABS

**FUN FACT:** GIANT RIVER OTTERS ARE SUCH FIERCE FIGHTERS THAT NOT EVEN A BLACK CAIMAN (PAGE 24) WOULD TRY TO CAPTURE ONE.

# BLACK CAIMAN

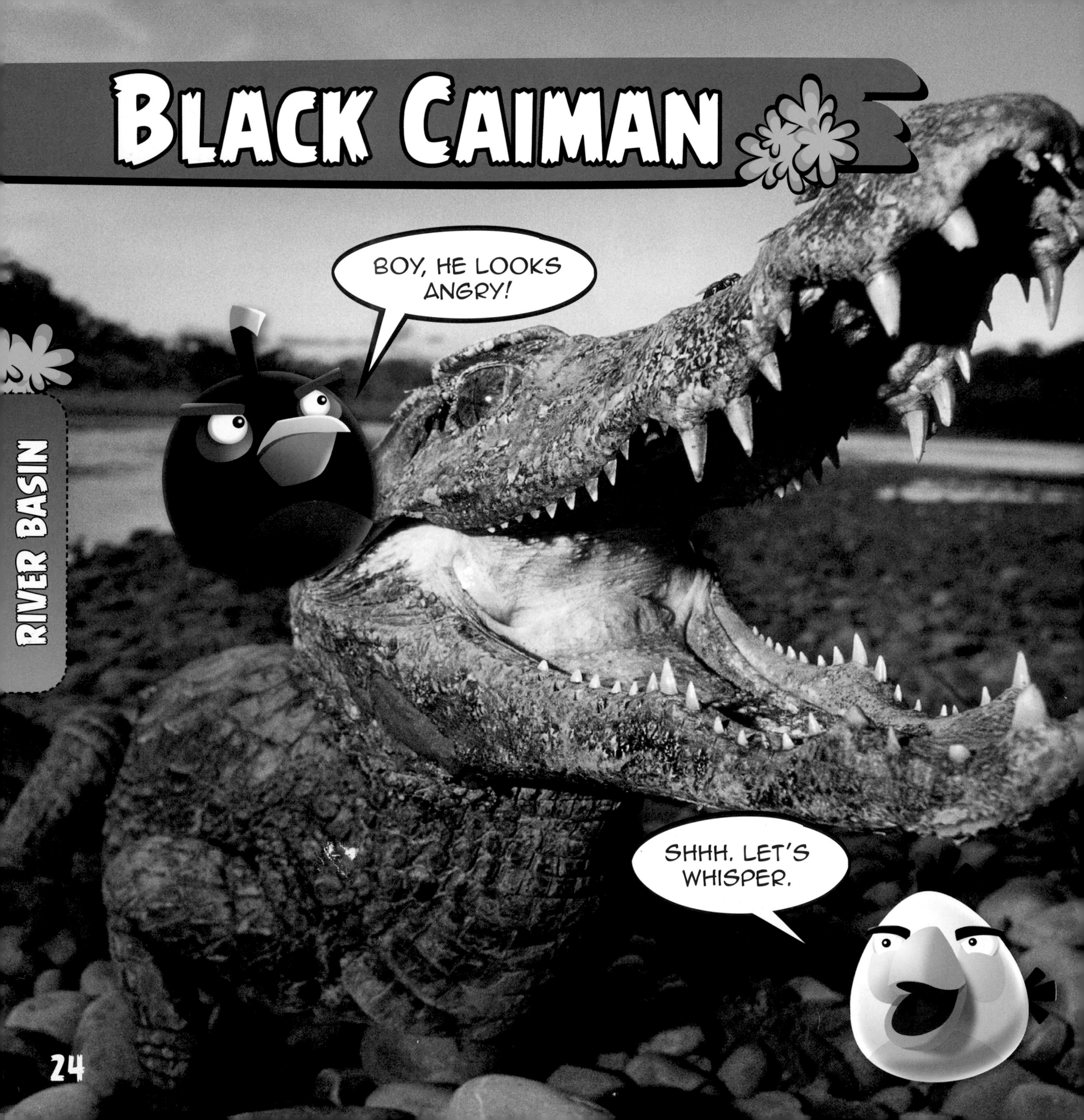

The sight of a black caiman strikes fear into any other animal in or near the water. This meat-eater's teeth are designed for grabbing, not chewing. So when this reptile captures prey, it pulls the animal into the water and drowns it, then swallows it whole.

When black caiman eggs hatch, the babies scurry away. That's good, because the adults sometimes eat their young.

Fully grown caimans need only fear humans, who hunt them for their leather and meat, and adult anaconda snakes, who hunt them for... well, dinner.

**SIZE: LENGTH:** 13 TO 20 FEET (4 TO 6 M) **WEIGHT:** 220 TO 1,102 POUNDS (100 TO 500 KG)

**ON THE MENU:** ANACONDAS, BIRDS, CAPYBARAS, DEER, FISH, TAPIRS, TURTLES

**FUN FACT:** THE BLACK CAIMAN IS THE LARGEST PREDATOR IN THE AMAZON.

# RED-BELLIED PIRANHA

RIVER BASIN

AWW, WOOK AT THE WITTLE FISHIES.

AREN'T THEY SWEET?

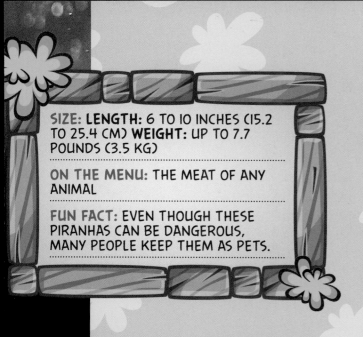

SIZE: **LENGTH:** 6 TO 10 INCHES (15.2 TO 25.4 CM) **WEIGHT:** UP TO 7.7 POUNDS (3.5 KG)

ON THE MENU: THE MEAT OF ANY ANIMAL

FUN FACT: EVEN THOUGH THESE PIRANHAS CAN BE DANGEROUS, MANY PEOPLE KEEP THEM AS PETS.

These river dwellers are famous for their giant appetites and razor-sharp teeth. When red-bellied piranhas are small, they eat fruits, plants, seeds, and other tiny water animals.

When they've grown to be an inch or two (2.5 to 5 cm) long, they bite the fins and flesh of other fish who get too close.

When they are fully grown, watch out! These fish swim in groups and sink their chompers into any animal foolish enough to invade their territory. Fishermen are careful not to dangle fingers or toes in piranha-infested waters.

SWEET? AWK! LET'S GET OUTTA HERE!

# TURTLES OF THE AMAZON

**RIVER BASIN**

The Amazon River and its tributaries (smaller streams flowing into it) are home to many other animals—like turtles. Turtles love slow-moving streams and swampy areas, where they can be seen on logs and rocks, basking in the sun, or sunk down so only their noses poke above the water's surface.

**MATA MATA**
The mata mata stands very still in shallow water, nose above the surface, looking like a piece of old bark. When a tasty-looking fish swims too close, the turtle opens its mouth wide and sucks it in like a living vacuum cleaner!

**SIZE: MATA MATA:** UP TO 18 INCHES (45 CM)/35 POUNDS (15.9 KG) **GIANT AMAZON RIVER TURTLE:** UP TO 30 INCHES (76 CM)/200 POUNDS (90.7 KG) **YELLOW-SPOTTED AMAZON RIVER TURTLE:** UP TO 18 INCHES (45 CM)/18 POUNDS (8.2 KG) **BIG-HEADED AMAZON RIVER TURTLE:** UP TO 9.3 INCHES (23.5 CM)/24.3 POUNDS (11 KG)

**ON THE MENU: MATA MATA:** FISH AND SMALL WATER ANIMALS **GIANT AMAZON RIVER TURTLE:** FALLEN FRUIT, INSECTS, PLANTS, SEEDS, SMALL WATER ANIMALS **YELLOW-SPOTTED AMAZON RIVER TURTLE:** FRUIT, WEEDS, FISH, SMALL WATER ANIMALS **BIG-HEADED AMAZON RIVER TURTLE:** FRUIT, SEEDS, FISH, WATER PLANTS, SMALL WATER ANIMALS

**FUN FACT:** A MATA MATA HAS A SKINNY, SNORKLE-LIKE BREATHING TUBE ON THE END OF ITS NOSE, PERFECT FOR A TURTLE WHO LIKES TO HIDE ITSELF DOWN IN THE WATER.

ALL I SEE IS A PILE OF DEAD LEAVES.

**GIANT AMAZON RIVER TURTLE**
One of the largest freshwater turtles in the world, these giants leave the water only to soak up a little sunshine or lay their eggs in the sand of a riverbank.

**YELLOW-SPOTTED AMAZON RIVER TURTLE**
Like the giant Amazon river turtle, these turtles are side-necked. When frightened, they bend their necks sideways—and tuck their heads under the front of their shells.

**BIG-HEADED AMAZON RIVER TURTLE**
A large head shaped like a triangle makes this turtle easy to recognize. Its shell has a high ridge straight down the center that wears down as the turtle gets older.

THAT'S THE TURTLE.

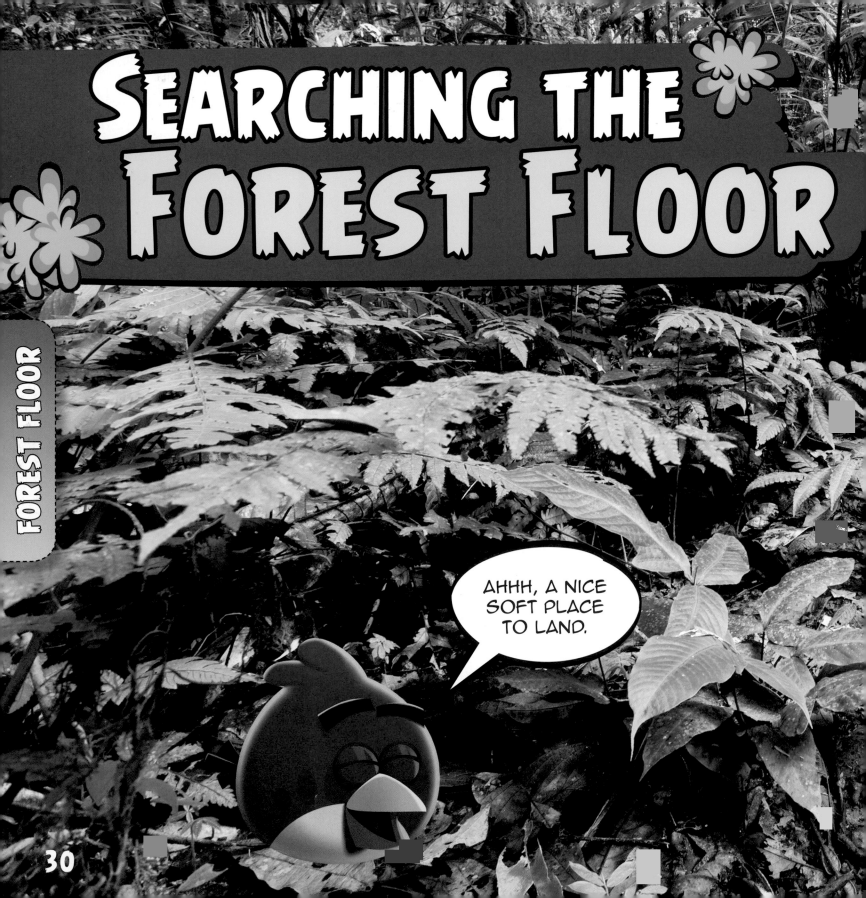

# SEARCHING THE FOREST FLOOR

THEY'D BETTER NOT BITE ME.

YEAH, HE'LL BITE BACK! KA-BOOM!

CAREFUL, LOTS OF BITING INSECTS LIVE HERE.

The forest floor is hot and damp. Dark, too, because trees growing above block almost all sunlight. A thick layer of fallen leaves and dead plants carpets the ground. As they decompose (rot), they become food for tree roots and insects.

31

**FOREST FLOOR**

Ferns grow here, as well as mushrooms and saplings (baby trees).

WORMS GROW HERE?

Tree roots don't go very deep, because the soil is poor. The top two inches (5 cm) of soil holds most of the nutrients (food) trees need to grow.

NO, FERNS. THOSE ARE PLANTS.

32

BUT WORMS GROW HERE, TOO!

## THE FOREST FLOOR

Leaves and fallen trees decompose quickly in this climate. Millions of insects help speed things up.

The Amazon rain forest is home to many animals that live nowhere else on Earth.

# CAPYBARA

FOREST FLOOR

Capybaras spend much of their time in the water—staying cool, eating plants, and avoiding predators like jaguars, caimans, and harpy eagles. Mornings and evenings, they come out to graze on grasses and reeds. Their webby feet leave behind star footprints.

Capybaras chirp to each other while grazing, and if a little capybara gets separated, its purrs and whistles mean "Help! Somebody find me!" When a predator nears, capybaras warn each other with sharp barks, all joining in until the danger passes. Sometimes, all that barking is enough to frighten away the predator. If not, the capybaras splash into the water and sink down so that only their ears, eyes, and nostrils show above the surface.

**SIZE: LENGTH:** 42 TO 53 INCHES (106 TO 134 CM) **WEIGHT:** 77.2 TO 145.5 POUNDS (35 TO 66 KG)

**ON THE MENU:** GRASSES, REEDS, WATER PLANTS

**FUN FACT:** CAPYBARAS EAT THEIR OWN POOP. THIS LETS THEIR BODIES USE NUTRIENTS THAT MAY HAVE...WELL, GONE THROUGH TOO QUICKLY THE FIRST TIME.

WAIT A MINUTE. THEY EAT WHAT?!

34

35

# AMAZON HORNED FROG

THAT MOUTH LOOKS BIG ENOUGH TO SWALLOW...

BIRDS!

BIRDS!

BIRDS!

SIZE: **LENGTH:** UP TO 8 INCHES (20 CM) **WEIGHT:** UP TO 1 POUND (.45 KG)

**ON THE MENU:** ANYTHING THAT FITS INTO ITS MOUTH

**FUN FACT:** AN AMAZON HORNED FROG WILL EVEN ATTACK A PASSING HUMAN.

This frog will attack and eat anything it can fit into its gigantic mouth. Snuggled down under fallen leaves, it waits patiently for a smaller animal to happen by, then...GOTCHA! Sharp teeth hold the unlucky prey in place until the frog swallows it whole—*gulp.*

Unless it can't. Sometimes, an Amazon horned frog's appetite is bigger than its mouth. They are often found dead with a too-big-to-swallow animal still stuck in their jaws. Now that's stubborn.

# GIANT ANTEATER

Anteaters have no teeth, but that doesn't stop them from eating as many as 35,000 ants every day. How? That tongue! The thing is two feet (0.6 m) long and covered with supersticky spit.

First, the anteater sniffs out an anthill on the rain forest floor. Then it tears in with its sharp, four-inch (10-cm)-long claws. It pokes its long snout into the opening, and —*shloop*—out comes the tongue, darting out and in, out and in. Ants are swallowed whole, and quickly, before they can sting. Baby anteaters often hitch a ride on their mom's back.

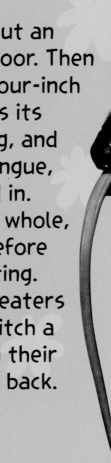

HEY, BOMB. IS MY TONGUE THAT LONG?

38

**SIZE: LENGTH:** 29 TO 42 INCHES (74 TO 107 CM) **WEIGHT:** 500 TO 800 POUNDS (227 TO 363 KG)

**ON THE MENU:** FRUIT, GRASSES, LEAVES, SEEDS

**FUN FACT:** AS A TAPIR ROAMS THE RAIN FOREST, IT'S HELPING GROW NEW TREES. HOW? IT'S SPREADING AROUND FRUIT SEEDS IN THE POOP IT DROPS.

AND PIRANHAS

AND ANACONDAS! OH MY!

This animal, with its grippy snout, is good at grabbing branches and picking fruit. No surprise there. But tapirs have another talent. Diving! They like being in the water, whether it's to cool off or go after tasty underwater plants or escape a predator.

Tapir toes are splayed—spread apart—to help them get across soft or muddy ground without sinking too far.

Baby tapirs have stripes on their backs that help them blend into the ground. That gives them a better chance against predators looking down from trees above, like jaguars or big snakes called anacondas. The stripes fade as the tapir grows bigger—and faster.

41

SIZE: **LENGTH:** UP TO 12 INCHES (30.5 CM) ACROSS **WEIGHT:** UP TO 2.5 OUNCES (70 G)

**ON THE MENU:** INSECTS, SMALL ANIMALS, BABY BIRDS, BABY RATS

**FUN FACT:** DESPITE HAVING EIGHT EYES, THESE SPIDERS CAN'T SEE VERY WELL. INSTEAD, THE HAIRS ON THEIR BODIES FEEL SMALL VIBRATIONS ON THE GROUND AND IN THE AIR.

KEEP YOUR DISTANCE, BIRDS.

Because of this big spider's name, you'd think it ate birds. But it only got that name because somebody long ago saw it eating a hummingbird (and that was probably a lucky catch). What this spider really likes is a good insect. Or a frog. Or a lizard or a bat or a snake. It isn't too picky.

Goliaths spend their days resting in damp underground burrows, then come out at night to crawl around. They sneak up on prey, grab it, and inject it with venom (poison). Then they drag or carry their catch back to their burrow, and...let the feast begin!

43

# Green Anaconda

FOREST FLOOR

Heaviest of all snakes, the green anaconda can't pull itself around very fast...on land. In water, it's a different story. They can strike so quickly that their prey—turtles, capybaras, caimans, and even jaguars—don't see them coming. That's because anacondas hide most of their bodies underwater, leaving only their eyes and noses peeking above the surface.

An anaconda watches...waits...then lunges, locking prey in its powerful jaws. The snake wraps its body around and around the animal and squeeeeezes. When the turtle or capybara or caiman is dead, the snake unhinges its jaws and swallows its prey whole, inch by inch.

WHY IS IT LOOKING AT US LIKE THAT?

44

SIZE: **LENGTH:** 20 TO 30 FEET (6 TO 9 M) **DIAMETER:** 12 INCHES (30 CM) **WEIGHT:** UP TO 550 POUNDS (227 KG)

**ON THE MENU:** CAIMANS, CAPYBARAS, DEER, FISH, TAPIRS, TURTLES, JAGUARS, WILD PIGS

**FUN FACT:** A GROUP OF ANACONDAS IS CALLED A BED OR A KNOT.

MAYBE IT WANTS A HUG.

NO, THANKS!

# LEAF-CUTTER ANT

FOREST FLOOR

THEIR LEAF MUSH WOULD BE WONDERFUL FOR MY GARDEN!

LENGTH: 0.1 TO 0.65 INCH (0.25 TO 1.65 CM)

ON THE MENU: A SPECIAL, HOMEMADE FUNGUS

FUN FACT: A COLONY MAY BE HOME TO AS MANY AS EIGHT MILLION ANTS!

Leaf-cutter ants are the gardeners of the rain forest. They hurry along, never out of line, hauling leaf snippets back to their underground nest. Back and forth, back and forth.

But the ants don't eat the leaves. They deliver them to others, whose job it is to chew them until they're soft and mushy, and then mix them with ant poop and place them in an underground room. These "gardens" are carefully tended until they grow a special fungus. This fungus is what feeds the entire colony.

UGH.

ARE YOU GOING TO MAKE US CHEW LEAVES?

# BUGS OF THE AMAZON

**FOREST FLOOR**

Scientists say that 90 percent of the animal species roaming the Amazon rain forest are insects—more than 2.5 million different kinds of them! They include ants and beetles, bees and wasps, butterflies and moths, cockroaches, crickets, grasshoppers, spiders, termites... every bug you can imagine and many you'd have to see to believe.

A MANTIS? I DON'T SEE IT.

ME, NEITHER.

**SIZE: SOUTH AMERICAN DEAD LEAF MANTIS:** 3 INCHES (7.5 CM) LONG **SPINY DEVIL KATYDID:** 2.5 TO 3 INCHES (6.4 TO 7.6 CM) LONG **VIOLET-WINGED GRASSHOPPER:** 6 INCHES (15 CM) LONG **HERCULES BEETLE:** 1.5 TO 6.7 INCHES (4 TO 17 CM) LONG

**ON THE MENU: SOUTH AMERICAN DEAD LEAF MANTIS:** INSECTS **SPINY DEVIL KATYDID:** UNKNOWN, BUT PROBABLY FLOWER PARTS, INSECTS, SEEDS **VIOLET-WINGED GRASSHOPPER:** PLANTS **HERCULES BEETLE:** DECAYING WOOD, FRUIT, LEAVES

**FUN FACT:** A HUMAN WITH THE SAME RELATIVE STRENGTH AS A HERCULES BEETLE COULD LIFT NINE ELEPHANTS!

**SOUTH AMERICAN DEAD LEAF MANTIS**
You can see how this mantis got its name. And guess what? When frightened, it lies very still or curls up and falls to the ground. Like a dead leaf!

48

**SPINY DEVIL KATYDID**
The spiny devil is a bold bug.
It uses its spiny front legs to
fight off hungry birds, bats,
and even monkeys!

**HERCULES BEETLE**
If one of these guys finds a
big stick blocking his path,
does he have to go around
it? Nope. This extremely
strong beetle uses his horn-
like pincers to move it out
of the way.

**VIOLET-WINGED GRASSHOPPER**
When this grasshopper flies by,
it might be mistaken for a bird.
It's that big—one of the largest
hoppers in the world, with a
sweeping wingspan of almost
9.5 inches (24 cm).

# UP TO THE ✿ UNDERSTORY!

IT'S HOT HERE.

YOU CAN USE LEAVES TO FAN YOURSELF!

The layer of rain forest plants and trees that grows above the forest floor, but not much higher than houses, is called the understory. The air feels hot and thick here. No breezes blow. Understory plants have large, wide leaves and grow so close together that it's hard to see—or walk—through them. Understory plants and trees are teeming with insects and other animal life.

## UNDERSTORY

Growls and howls. Squawks and screeches. Chitters and chirps and clicks and croaks. The rain forest is never quiet.

HOPE WE DON'T GET CAUGHT IN A WEB.

The understory is a great place for spiders to capture insects. They stretch webs across well-traveled flight paths, from leaf to leaf or branch to branch.

THAT WOULD MAKE ME ANGRY.

52

# THE UNDERSTORY

Flowers and fruits growing here are pale, brightly colored, or strong-smelling. This makes them easier to see in the dim light—and easier for animals to find.

MMM, CHOCOLATE.

Banana plants, cacao trees (we make chocolate from cacao seeds), and the umbrella-shaped cecropia are all common in the understory.

# JAGUAR

No rain forest animal wants to meet up with a jaguar, because most of them are on the big cat's menu. Unfortunately for them, jaguars are as comfortable in understory trees as they are on the ground. They sit on a branch, watching the trail below. When an animal passes underneath—*whomp!*—the big jag pounces.

And nobody's safe in the water, either. These spotted cats like to splash around!

**SIZE: HEAD AND BODY:** 5 TO 6 FEET (1.5 TO 1.8 M) LONG **TAIL:** 27.5 TO 36 INCHES (70 TO 91 CM) LONG **WEIGHT:** 100 TO 250 POUNDS (45 TO 113 KG)

**ON THE MENU:** DEER, CAPYBARAS, MONKEYS, REPTILES, SLOTHS, TAPIRS, FISH, TURTLES

**FUN FACT:** THE WORD "JAGUAR" COMES FROM THE NATIVE AMERICAN WORD *YAGUAR*, WHICH MEANS "HE WHO KILLS WITH ONE LEAP."

# CAPUCHIN MONKEY

CRUSHED MILLIPEDE KEEPS MOSQUITOES AWAY?

SIZE: **LENGTH:** 12 TO 22 INCHES (30 TO 56 CM) **TAIL:** AS LONG AS THE BODY **WEIGHT:** 3 TO 9 POUNDS (1.36 TO 4.9 KG)

**ON THE MENU:** FRUITS, NUTS, SEEDS, BIRD EGGS, FROGS, INSECTS, LIZARDS, SPIDERS

**FUN FACT:** CAPUCHINS CRUSH MILLIPEDES AND SMEAR THE MUSH ON THEIR FUR TO KEEP MOSQUITOES FROM BITING.

If capuchins are awake, they're probably searching for food. That's why the understory is a favorite hangout. Here, bananas are plentiful, and cacao seedpods hide one of this monkey's favorite treats—the sweet fruit inside.

Capuchins are smart. They know they're safer in the trees than on the ground. So when they need a drink of water, they come down very, very carefully. Even when they're eating, they're watching for jaguars, snakes, and large birds of prey.

I'D RATHER HAVE MOSQUITO BITES.

57

# MARGAY

See those big eyes? Those give a clue that the margay is a night hunter. This small cat rarely leaves the trees. It sleeps there, eats there, and spends its nights leaping from branch to branch, chasing the birds and lizards and monkeys it likes to eat.

Margays are terrific climbers. Their back paws grab branches as easily as their front paws do. Most cats inch down tree trunks backward. Not this one. The margay runs straight down a tree trunk like a squirrel. It can even hang from a branch by one foot.

MONKEYS SOUND LIKE THIS: OOH. OOH. OOH.

**SIZE: LENGTH:** 19 TO 31 INCHES (48 TO 79 CM) **WEIGHT:** 9 TO 20 POUNDS (4.1 TO 9.1 KG)

**ON THE MENU:** BIRDS, EGGS, FROGS, LIZARDS, SMALL MONKEYS, RATS, SLOTHS, SQUIRRELS

**FUN FACT:** MARGAYS CAN MAKE BABY TAMARIN MONKEY SOUNDS. WHEN AN ADULT TAMARIN COMES TO INVESTIGATE, THE MARGAY TRIES TO CAPTURE IT.

58

59

# Emerald Tree Boa Constrictor

**SIZE: LENGTH:** 5 TO 6.5 FEET (1.5 TO 2 M) **WEIGHT:** 2.4 TO 3.3 POUNDS (1.1 TO 1.5 KG)

**ON THE MENU:** BIRDS, FROGS, LIZARDS, RODENTS

**FUN FACT:** EMERALD TREE BOAS CAN HANG UPSIDE DOWN BY THEIR TAILS. SOMETIMES THEY EAT THAT WAY.

This snake's bright green skin is outstanding camouflage. That's good for sneaking up on prey like birds and lizards. But it's also good for hiding from enemies. Even a sharp-eyed harpy eagle looking for a snaky snack might have a hard time finding one of these among the leaves.

Emerald tree boas rest during the day, curled up on a branch. They hunt at night, moving quickly from tree to tree. They grab branches with their tails to keep from falling.

Like the anaconda, this snake is a constrictor. That means it wraps its body around its unlucky prey and squeezes until the animal can no longer breathe.

WHY?

BECAUSE AFTER HE SWALLOWS—

IT HAS TO GO AROUND AND AROUND AND AROUND!

# GREATER BULLDOG BAT

**SIZE: LENGTH:** 4.6 TO 5 INCHES (10.9 TO 12.7 CM) **WINGSPAN:** 3 FEET (1 M) **WEIGHT:** 1.8 TO 3.2 OUNCES (50 TO 90 G)

**ON THE MENU:** FISH, BEETLES, MOTHS, SHRIMP, CRABS

**FUN FACT:** THE GREATER BULLDOG BAT CAN SWIM, USING ITS BIG WINGS TO PADDLE.

WHAT'S OUR WINGSPAN, RED?

This bat's pushed-in nose makes it look like a bulldog. It is one of the few bats known to capture and eat fish. How? When fish are swimming near the surface, this bat can sense ripples on the water by using echolocation (bat radar). Other times it flies over a spot where fish have been jumping, raking the surface with its sharp, curved claws. It catches a fish in those claws, then moves it up to its mouth. The bat can eat the fish while flying or find a perch to enjoy its feast.

This large bat flaps slowly along with a wingspan of three feet (1 m).

WE DON'T HAVE WINGS, CHUCK.

DOESN'T MATTER. WE'VE GOT THE SLINGSHOT.

# HOATZIN

The bad news? These birds are odd-looking, clumsy, terrible fliers that make weird croaking, grunting, hissing noises. And their nickname? Stinkbird. You can guess why.

The good news? Nobody wants to eat them.

Monkeys will eat hoatzin eggs, though. And large birds of prey will eat their chicks. That's why hoatzin parents build their platform nests on limbs that hang over the water. If chicks are under attack, they can drop into the water and swim to a safer place. Then they can climb back up to the nest later. Yes, climb. A hoatzin chick has two claws on the front edge of each wing. No fooling.

SIZE: **LENGTH:** UP TO 26 INCHES (65 CM) **WINGSPAN:** 35 TO 39.3 INCHES (90 TO 100 CM) **WEIGHT:** 1.6 TO 1.98 POUNDS (0.7 TO 1 KG)

**ON THE MENU:** LEAVES, SHOOTS, AND BUDS; A FEW FLOWERS AND FRUITS

**FUN FACT:** THE HOATZIN'S DIGESTIVE SYSTEM IS MORE COW-LIKE THAN BIRDLIKE. NO WONDER THE LEAVES THEY EAT COME OUT SMELLING LIKE COW MANURE.

# POISON DART FROGS

THEY'RE COLORFUL, LIKE US!

**LENGTH:** 1 TO 2.5 INCHES (2.5 TO 6.35 CM)

**ON THE MENU:** ANTS, TERMITES, TINY INSECTS, AND SPIDERS

**FUN FACT:** ONLY ONE ANIMAL CAN EAT POISON DART FROGS SAFELY, AND THAT IS A SNAKE WITH A NAME AS LONG AS ITS BODY: *LEIMADOPHIS EPINEPHELUS.*

These frogs look like they fell out of a rainbow. But their bright colors are a warning to other animals that these little cuties are poison. If another animal eats one, that animal will become paralyzed (unable to move), become sick, or even croak (and not in a good way).

To become parents, a froggy pair chooses a leaf and both clean it before the female lays her eggs. Then the father eggsits, careful to keep the eggs from drying out. After they hatch, the tiny tadpoles swim up onto their father's back. He carries them to a safe, watery place to grow bigger. Giddyup, Pop!

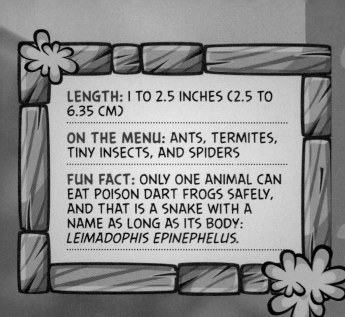

BUT THEY AREN'T ANGRY.

OH, WELL. YOU CAN'T HAVE EVERYTHING.

# AMAZONIAN SPIDERS

**L**ike insects, spiders can be found in all layers of the rain forest. They are tiny—or bigger than your head. They live in colonies of thousands—or alone. They build enormous webs—or make sticky webbing to fling at prey. They live in trees. On the ground. And underground.

So many different kinds of spiders live in the Amazon rain forest that humans will likely never discover them all.

**BRAZILIAN WANDERING SPIDER** *(PHONEUTRIA FERA)* This spider doesn't waste time building a web. It wanders the dark rain forest floor, chasing down and attacking insects. It is fast and poisonous and will bite humans.

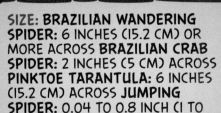

SIZE: **BRAZILIAN WANDERING SPIDER:** 6 INCHES (15.2 CM) OR MORE ACROSS **BRAZILIAN CRAB SPIDER:** 2 INCHES (5 CM) ACROSS **PINKTOE TARANTULA:** 6 INCHES (15.2 CM) ACROSS **JUMPING SPIDER:** 0.04 TO 0.8 INCH (1 TO 22 MM) ACROSS

ON THE MENU: INSECTS

WE'RE NOT CRAZY ABOUT SPIDERS.

**PINKTOE TARANTULA**
**(CAVICULARIA AVICULARIA)**
Common in the Amazon, the gentle pinktoe is a sit-and-wait hunter, not dangerous to humans. This hairy tree dweller changes from pink to black as it grows.

**JUMPING SPIDERS**
**(SALTICIDAE FAMILY)**
This itsy-bitsy spider has excellent eyesight. That helps it zero in on prey as it leaps from a tree and floats down, dangling from a "rope" of silk that comes out of its rear end.

DON'T WORRY, THESE AREN'T BIRD-EATERS.

**BRAZILIAN CRAB SPIDER**
**(EPICADUS HETEROGASTER)**
White, purple, bright yellow ...the amazing crab spider changes color to make bees and butterflies think it's part of a flower. When they get close, the spider pounces.

69

# THE CONCEALING CANOPY

NOW, THIS IS MORE LIKE IT.

WHO LIVES HERE, MATILDA?

rees growing at the canopy level act like a roof over the understory and forest floor. Branches and leaves grow so close together that they block most sunlight and rainfall from getting through to the layers below. They provide homes—and food—for animals as tiny as tree frogs and as large as howler monkeys.

# LOOKING AT THE LAYERS:
# THE CANOPY

CANOPY

Many trees here have pointed leaves so water can drip off quickly.

VERY COOL.

THE CANOPY

HE WAS TALKING ABOUT THE PLANTS HERE, BOMB.

Many animals living here never come down to the ground.

Thick, twisting vines called lianas climb up tree trunks, reaching for sunlight.

COOL? I'M HOT.

Flowers, ferns, and mosses grow piggyback on canopy trees.

# GREAT POTOO

A potoo's hunting style: Blend into a tree and don't...move...a muscle. It works, too. These birds are almost impossible to spot until dark, when their big orange eyes reflect the moonlight.

But they have a special trick to keep that from happening. They have slits in their eyelids, so they can see something moving without opening their eyes all the way. When a moth or beetle or grasshopper flies by, the potoo darts from its perch and captures supper in its superwide mouth.

74

SIZE: **LENGTH:** 19 TO 24 INCHES (48 TO 60 CM) **WINGSPAN:** UP TO 39 INCHES (99 CM) **WEIGHT:** UP TO 1.4 POUNDS (.63 KG)

**ON THE MENU:** MOTHS AND OTHER LARGE FLYING INSECTS

**FUN FACT:** WHEN A POTOO IS STARTLED, IT MAKES A SUDDEN, LOUD BARK THAT SOUNDS LIKE *BWOW!* OR *GWOK!*

75

# TOUCAN



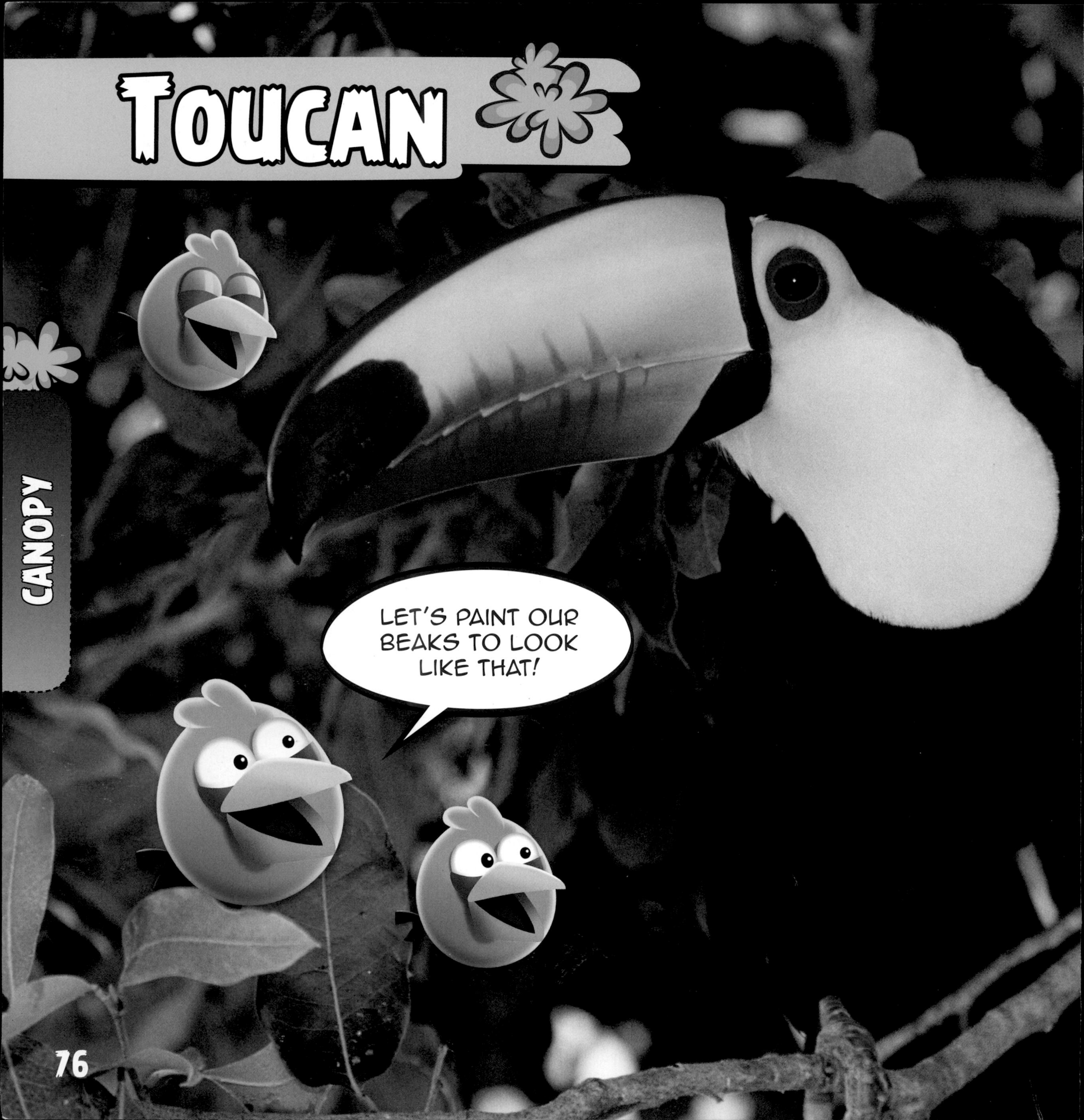

SIZE: **LENGTH:** 7 INCHES TO 2 FEET (18 TO 64 CM) **WINGSPAN:** 20 TO 47 INCHES (50 TO 119 CM) **WEIGHT:** 1.25 POUNDS (.57 KG)

**ON THE MENU:** MOSTLY FRUIT

**FUN FACT:** TOUCANS LIKE TO PLAY CATCH WITH EACH OTHER, TOSSING BITS OF FRUIT.

A toucan's colorful bill looks heavy, but it is actually lightweight, made of the same stuff as human fingernails. With a handy bill like this, a toucan has no trouble plucking hard-to-reach fruit or tossing tasty bites back into its throat.

Toucans are squawky creatures, calling noisily back and forth to their friends. When they aren't eating, playful toucans might enjoy a game of beak wrestling.

OUR BEAKS ARE TOO SHORT.

# KINKAJOU

CANOPY

Since they rest in treetops during the day, it's tough to spot kinkajous. But their barking and screeching is a familiar Amazon sound. These night hunters are often called honey bears. Can you guess their favorite food? Yep, honey. They just reach their long tongues into a beehive and slurp out the sweet treat. Bees might get mad, but it's probably hard to sting a kinkajou through such thick fur.

Those tongues are good for scooping nectar from flowers, too. And even for licking up termites.

Kinkajous have long, grippy tails they can hang from. And their sharp-clawed feet—that can twist around backward!—are perfect for scampering through the trees. Change direction? No problem. Up, down, left, right, right, left.

I LIKE SAYING "KINKAJOU."

78

# GOLDEN LION TAMARIN

These fiery-haired little monkeys sleep at night and hunt by day. They poke their long fingers into holes and cracks in trees searching for insects. If a lizard passes too close, they'll eat him, too.

Tamarins have a special alarm call when they see a large bird flying above. Since nobody wants to get eaten, neighboring tamarins find a hiding place, quick!

Unlike their monkey relatives (and humans), tamarins don't have flat fingernails. Theirs are claw-like, better for clinging to branches and tree trunks.

**SIZE: HEAD AND BODY:** 7.5 TO 8.75 INCHES (19 TO 22 CM) LONG **TAIL:** 10.25 TO 13.5 INCHES (26 TO 34 CM) LONG **WEIGHT:** UP TO 1.3 POUNDS (.6 KG)

**ON THE MENU:** BIRDS, FRUIT, INSECTS, LIZARDS

**FUN FACT:** GOLDEN LION TAMARINS MIGHT LOOK BIG IN PICTURES, BUT THEY ARE ONLY ABOUT THE SIZE OF A FIVE-YEAR-OLD CHILD'S FOOT.

81

# HOWLER MONKEY

CANOPY

THEY'RE TOO LOUD!

THAT MAKES ME ANGRY!

SIZE: **HEAD AND BODY:** 22 TO 36 INCHES (56 TO 91 CM) LONG **TAIL:** 23 TO 36 INCHES (58 TO 91 CM) LONG **WEIGHT:** 15 TO 22 POUNDS (7 TO 10 KG)

ON THE MENU: LEAVES, FLOWERS, FRUIT

FUN FACT: IF A HOWLER FALLS FROM A BRANCH, ITS STRONG TAIL CAN GRAB ANOTHER ON THE WAY DOWN AND SAVE IT. PHEW!

If you're looking for THE LOUDEST ANIMAL IN THE AMAZON, you've found it. When a group of these monkeys starts howling—in the morning and again before bedtime—they can be heard up to three miles (4.8 km) away!

Those deep, roaring howls aren't just for the fun of it, though. Howlers call out to let other howlers know where they are. It's their way of avoiding fights, of saying, "This is our territory. So, the rest of you? Stay away!" Far-off howlers howl right back, their way of saying, "Yeah, yeah. We hear you!"

Howlers aren't just the loudest monkeys in the Amazon, they're also the biggest.

JUST COVER YOUR EARS.

# BLACK-HANDED SPIDER MONKEY

CANOPY

When four hands aren't enough, use your...tail? You can, if you're a spider monkey. The end of this monkey's tail has ridged skin, so it can grip branches and pick fruit and even throw things as easily as a hand can.

Everything spider monkeys need is up in the trees—food, shelter, friends—so they rarely come down.

Until it's a year old, a little monkey rides around on its mama's back. Then it begins exploring away from her with a group of other young monkeys. They practice calling and grunting to each other, and if a jaguar or harpy eagle nears, they yap-yap-yap a warning.

WOW. IT'S LIKE THEY HAVE FIVE HANDS.

SIZE: **HEAD AND BODY:** UNDER 12 TO ALMOST 25 INCHES (30 TO 63 CM) LONG **TAIL:** 23 TO 29 INCHES (58 TO 74 CM) LONG **WEIGHT:** UP TO 13 POUNDS (6 KG)

**ON THE MENU:** FRUIT, SEEDS, NUTS, LEAVES, INSECTS, BIRD EGGS

**FUN FACT:** BABY SPIDER MONKEYS DON'T HOLD HANDS WITH THEIR MAMAS. THEY HOLD TAILS.

WE'D LIKE FIVE HANDS.

I'D LIKE ONE HAND.

# SQUIRREL MONKEY

THEY WATCH OUT FOR EACH OTHER.

These monkeys are about the size of Barbie dolls. They stay alert and stick close to the middle of the canopy layer. Any higher, and they risk being eaten by an eagle or hawk. On the ground, they might be eaten by a prowling cat or an anaconda.

They're omnivores. That means they'll eat plants or small animals, whatever's handy. During the day, they hunt in groups. They have terrific eyesight, so spotting brightly colored fruit is easy for them. At night, groups come together to feel safer. Sleeping groups might have 50, 100, or as many as 500 monkeys in them!

These monkeys don't have grippy tails, so they have to use their hands to climb or swing from branch to branch.

LIKE WE DO!

SIZE: **HEAD AND BODY:** 10 TO 14 INCHES (25 TO 36 CM) LONG **TAIL:** 14 TO 18 INCHES (35 TO 42 CM) LONG **WEIGHT:** UP TO 2.5 POUNDS (1.1 KG)

**ON THE MENU:** FRUIT, BERRIES, FLOWERS, LEAVES, SEEDS, TREE GUM, LIZARDS

**FUN FACT:** SCIENTISTS SAY THESE SMART LITTLE MONKEYS USE 26 DIFFERENT CALLS TO COMMUNICATE WITH ONE ANOTHER.

# GLASS FROG

CANOPY

This little frog's color is a perfect match for the leaves where it lives. That's good for hiding from animals that would eat it, like snakes and birds.

But underneath this frog is something it can't hide—its insides! The skin over its belly is see-through, as clear as...well, glass. You can see its tiny heart beating, bump-bump-bump, as well as—in some frogs—green bones!

Glass frogs are night hunters with excellent eyesight. When one spots a juicy-looking fly, it leaps forward, mouth open, to capture it. Gulp. Goodbye, fly!

**LENGTH:** 1 TO 3 INCHES (2.5 TO 8 CM)

**ON THE MENU:** FLIES AND OTHER SMALL SOFT-BODIED INSECTS, SPIDERS

**FUN FACT:** FEMALE GLASS FROGS LAY THEIR EGGS ON A LEAF ABOVE A STREAM. WHEN THE TADPOLES HATCH, THEY JUST DROP INTO THE WATER TO FINISH GROWING.

YOU CAN SEE HIS GUTS!

89

# SCARLET IBIS

**SIZE: LENGTH:** 30 INCHES (75 CM) **WINGSPAN:** 21 INCHES (54 CM) **WEIGHT:** UP TO 3 POUNDS (1.4 KG)

**ON THE MENU:** SHRIMP AND OTHER CRUSTACEANS, FISH, FROGS, INSECTS, SNAKES

**FUN FACT:** LIKE GEESE, SCARLET IBISES FLY IN A V-FORMATION. WHEN THE LEADER GETS TIRED, IT FALLS BACK AND LETS ANOTHER TAKE ITS PLACE.

THE REDDER THEY ARE, THE OLDER THEY ARE?

Check out those long legs. Perfect for wading! And if you had to poke for shrimp or tadpoles in squishy mud or underwater, wouldn't you be glad for such a long curved bill?

It's the kind of food they eat that makes these birds an eye-popping red. They're grayish brown when young. So the redder the bird, the older it is.

Ibises feed and fly and nest in groups called flocks. Their nests are loose, built high in trees where eggs and chicks will be safe from predators.

BOY, RED, YOU MUST BE ANCIENT.

YOU'RE SO FUNNY I FORGOT TO LAUGH.

# THREE-TOED SLOTH

**M**eet the slowest animal on Earth. How slow? So slow that tiny green plants called algae grow on its furry coat. But, hey, blending into the leaves is a good thing when your neighbors are hungry eagles and jaguars.

Sloths can climb quickly when they need to. They'd rather not, that's all. Their long, strong claws help them hold on tightly while napping upside down. And eating upside down. And even having babies upside down.

Coming to the ground is dangerous for a sloth. Its back legs are weak, so it has to dig in with its front claws and drag itself forward awkwardly. In water, it's a different story. Sloths are smooth, strong swimmers.

**SIZE: LENGTH:** UP TO 23 INCHES (58 CM)
**WEIGHT:** UP TO 8.75 POUNDS (4 KG)

**ON THE MENU:** LEAVES AND MORE LEAVES

**FUN FACT:** SINCE SLOTHS GIVE BIRTH HANGING UPSIDE DOWN, A NEWBORN BABY HAS TO GRAB ON TO ITS MOTHER'S FUR AND HOLD TIGHT TO KEEP FROM FALLING!

HE LOOKS HAPPY. MAYBE WE CAN BE FRIENDS?

93

# Green Iguana

WHA-? THEIR TAILS CAN TEAR OFF?

AND THEY'LL GROW BACK?

94

SIZE: **LENGTH:** UP TO 6.6 FEET (2 M) **WEIGHT:** 11 POUNDS (5 KG)

ON THE MENU: LEAVES, FLOWERS, FRUIT

FUN FACT: LIKE ITS SMALLER LIZARD COUSINS, AN IGUANA'S TAIL CAN TEAR OFF, THEN SLOWLY GROW BACK.

**D**espite their name, green iguanas aren't always green. Their knobby skin can be shades of brown or tan or red or blue, and it can be patterned with blotches or stripes. Their skin color can even change, depending on what they eat and where they're living.

Iguanas enjoy hanging out in trees near water and are excellent swimmers. See those thick, sharp tails? They use those like whips to drive off predators.

If something frightens an iguana, its first choice is to run away. But it might choose to escape by diving off a branch into the water below—or even onto solid ground. *Thwump.* Ouch.

NOT RIGHT AWAY, BUT YES.

# LIZARDS IN THE RAIN FOREST

CANOPY

The Amazon region is home to more than 100 kinds of lizards of different sizes and shapes, with different styles of hunting and different diets. They're found everywhere in the rain forest region—near creeks and streams, scampering over the forest floor, and clinging to twigs high in the canopy.

THEY'RE EVERYWHERE!

**TURNIP-TAILED GECKO**
This gecko is a night hunter. Its chubby tail stores fat and can tear off when grabbed by a predator, allowing the gecko to escape.

**NORTHERN CAIMAN LIZARD**
The colorful caiman divides its time between trees and water. Its powerful jaws are perfect for cracking open snail shells to get at the gooey treat inside.

**BRIDLED FOREST GECKO**
Also a tree dweller, this little gecko isn't a chaser. It would rather sit perfectly still and wait. Sooner or later, a tasty insect or caterpillar comes crawling along.

**SIZE: NORTHERN CAIMAN LIZARD:** 2 TO 4 FEET (60 TO 121 CM) LONG **TURNIP-TAILED GECKO:** 4.7 INCHES (12 CM) LONG **BRIDLED FOREST GECKO:** 2.4 TO 3.2 INCHES (6 TO 8 CM) LONG **BANDED TREE ANOLE:** 10 INCHES (25 CM) LONG

**ON THE MENU: NORTHERN CAIMAN LIZARD:** SNAILS, INSECTS, FISH, CRABS, RODENTS **TURNIP-TAILED GECKO:** INSECTS, CATERPILLARS, SPIDERS **BRIDLED FOREST GECKO:** INSECTS AND CATERPILLARS **BANDED TREE ANOLE:** INSECTS

**FUN FACT:** TURNIP-TAILED GECKOS HAVE FLAPS OF SKIN GROWING ALONG THEIR BODIES. WHEN ONE JUMPS OUT OF A TREE, THESE FLAPS ACT LIKE PARACHUTES TO SLOW THE ANIMAL'S FALL.

**BANDED TREE ANOLE**
This blue-eyed lizard spends its entire life in trees. If it isn't resting, it's running after crunchy ants and beetles and cockroaches.

97

# EXPLORING THE EMERGENT

WOW, YOU CAN SEE FOREVER FROM THESE TREES.

THAT'S WHY BIRDS LOVE IT UP HERE.

Trees that poke up here and there above the canopy are called emergent. Towering 200 feet (60 m) or more into the sky, these giants have to be tough to survive all kinds of weather. Blistering sun. Harsh winds. Pelting rain. Their limbs are gnarled, their leaves smaller and fewer.

# Looking at the Layers:
# THE EMERGENT

## EMERGENT

## THE EMERGENT

Common emergent layer trees are the Brazil nut, cuipo, and kapok.

Scientists tested some of these giant trees and discovered that they were more than 1,000 years old.

HURRY UP, BIRDS.

YEAH, I WANNA SEE WHO GETS TO LIVE UP HERE.

While trees at lower layers count on animals and birds to spread their seeds, most emergent trees have winged or fluffy seeds, so the wind can carry them away.

Many animals climb or fly between the canopy and emergent layers. Some are hunting tasty insects. Some are seeking fruits, nuts, and seeds. Others are nesting—or simply looking for a safe place to sleep.

101

# COATIMUNDI



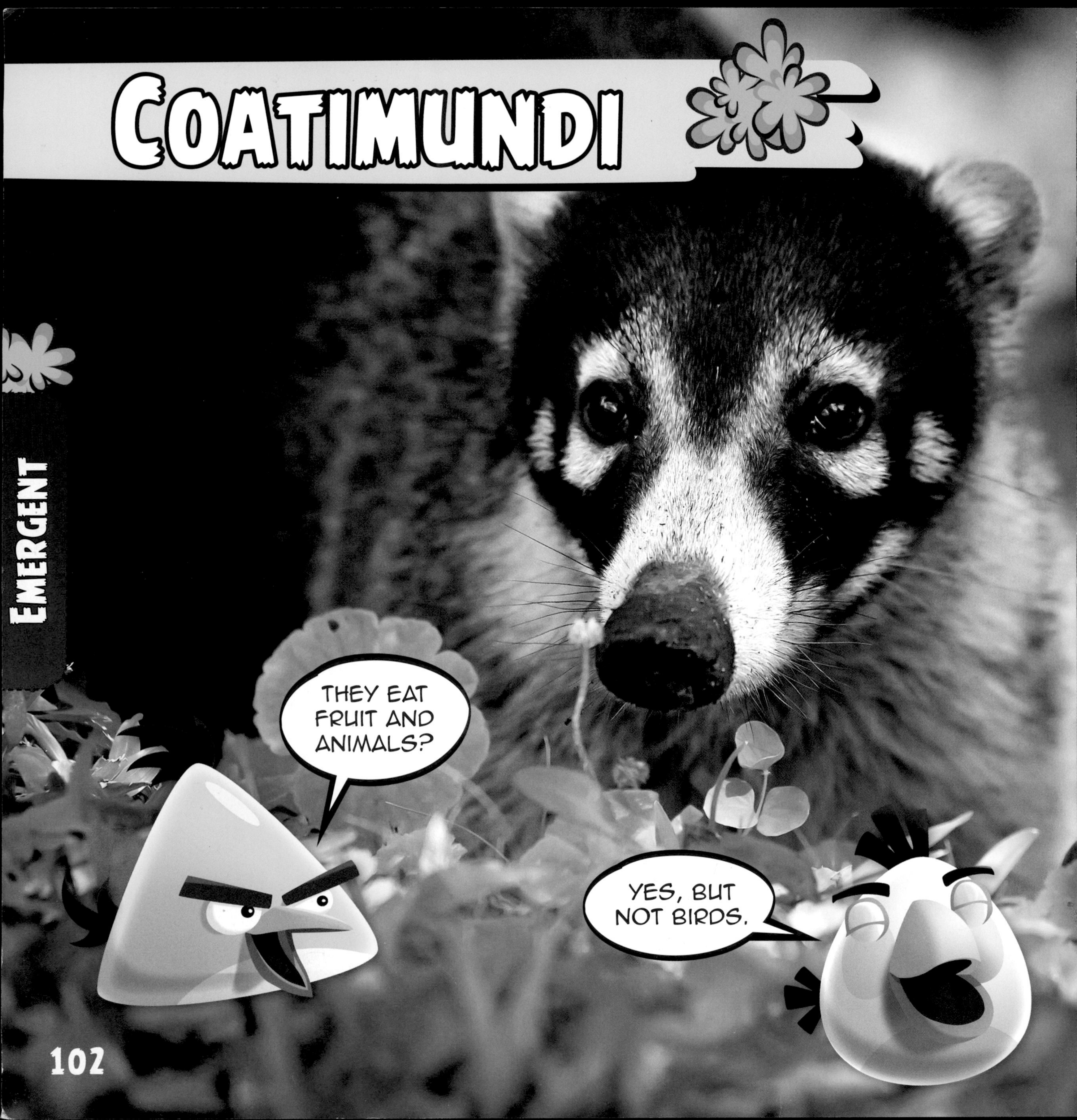

Think this ring-tailed animal might be another raccoon relative? You're right!

Those long tails are special. They help the animal balance when climbing through all levels of the rain forest and help family members find one another in tall grass.

A group of coatis is called a band. They don't play music, but they do click and squeak. They spend lots of time hunting, sticking their noses under rocks and into every kind of opening. Long claws are good for digging holes and tearing into rotting logs. What are coatis looking for? Fruit is their favorite treat. If they can't find that, insects or lizards or frogs will do.

**SIZE: BODY:** UP TO 24 INCHES (60 CM) LONG **TAIL:** UP TO 24 INCHES (60 CM) LONG **WEIGHT:** UP TO 18 POUNDS (8 KG)

**ON THE MENU:** FRUIT AND BERRIES, INSECTS, SMALL ANIMALS LIKE FROGS AND LIZARDS, EGGS

**FUN FACT:** WHEN A BAND OF COATIS IS STARTLED, THEY WOOF-WOOF-WOOF AND RACE TO SCRAMBLE BACK UP INTO THE TREES!

I SHOULD HOPE NOT!

103

# HARPY EAGLE

**T**alk about patient. These birds can sit without moving for hours...waiting... waiting. But when the right meal appears, watch out! Harpy eagles can dive as fast as 50 miles an hour (about 80 km/h) to snatch a monkey or sloth or green iguana from a branch.

Would carrying a struggling animal be tricky? Not for these birds. Their feet are as big as a person's hands, and those curved claws are five inches (12.7 cm) long.

Powerful wings help them twist and turn up through the trees to their nests. Those are built of sticks, leaves, and animal furs and are four feet (1.2 m) thick and five feet (1.5 m) across.

**EMERGENT**

TAKE IT EASY, BIG FELLAS.

104

SIZE: **LENGTH:** 35 TO 41 INCHES (89 CM TO 1.04 M) **WINGSPAN:** 6.5 TO 7 FEET (2 TO 2.13 M) **WEIGHT:** UP TO 20 POUNDS (9 KG)

**ON THE MENU:** SLOTHS, MONKEYS, OPOSSUMS, SOME REPTILES AND BIRDS

**FUN FACT:** WHEN A HARPY EAGLE IS ALERT OR UPSET, FEATHERS STAND STRAIGHT UP ATOP ITS HEAD.

# RED UAKARI

THERE'S SOMETHING ABOUT HIS FACE THAT I LIKE.

HOW DO YOU SAY THEIR NAME?

106

SIZE: LENGTH: 14 TO 22.5 INCHES (36 TO 57 CM) WEIGHT: 4.4 TO 6.6 POUNDS (2 TO 3 KG)

ON THE MENU: FRUIT, LEAVES, INSECTS, NECTAR, NUTS, SEEDS

FUN FACT: UNLIKE OTHER MONKEYS, RED UAKARIS HAVE SHORT, STUBBY TAILS.

A red uakari's eyes almost appear to be looking out through a rubbery mask. These cat-size monkeys live in flooded forests or near rivers and lakes. They spend most of their time in the treetops. If the weather has been very dry, they'll come to the ground to eat roots and seeds.

During the day, red uakaris roam the canopy, looking for fruit, leaves, and insects to eat. At night, they climb to the treetops and sleep in large groups.

While searching for food, a mother red uakari talks to her young with a hic-hic-hic call. Her little ones hic-hic-hic back to let her know where they are.

WAH-KAR-EE

# King Vulture



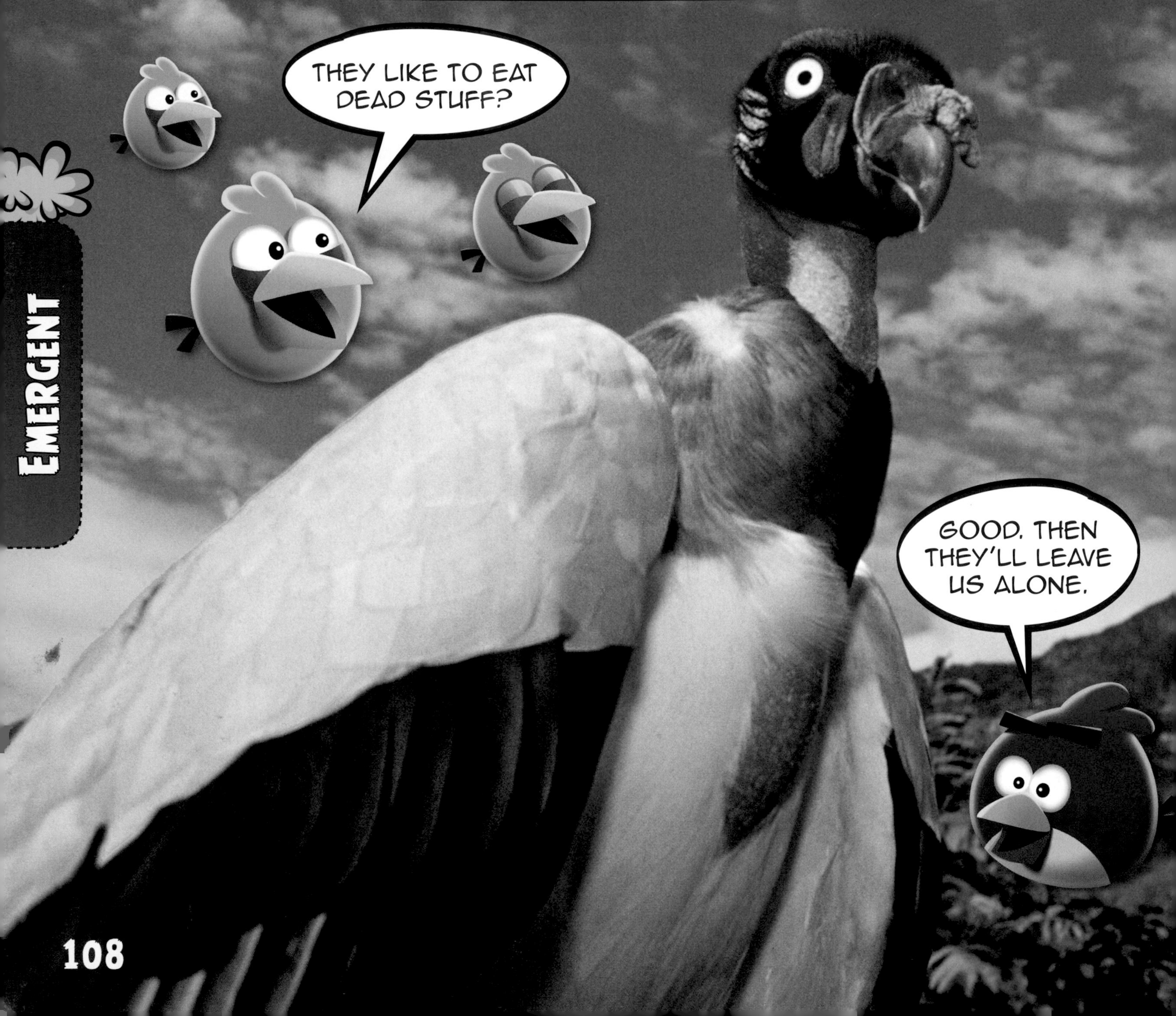

STILL. I'VE GOT YOUR BACK, GUYS.

Colorful king vultures aren't picky eaters. Fresh food? Nope, not their style. Some other predator's leftovers? Yeah, that's more like it!

They soar high above the rain forest or perch in treetops, waiting and watching. Sooner or later, they see a jaguar or other predator make a kill. They watch...and wait... and when the predator has eaten its fill, guess who drops in for his share?

SIZE: LENGTH: 27 TO 32 INCHES (67 TO 80 CM) WINGSPAN: 5 FEET (1.5 M) WEIGHT: 6 TO 10 POUNDS (2.7 TO 4.5 KG)

ON THE MENU: DEAD ANIMALS

FUN FACT: WHEN THE KING SHOWS UP AT A FOOD SITE, EVERY OTHER BIRD IMMEDIATELY BACKS OFF.

# MANY MACAWS

**EMERGENT**

**W**hat would the Amazon rain forest be without these large, squawking birds? They are seen—and heard—almost everywhere. There are many different kinds of macaws, all with different-colored feathers and different habits. Here are just a few.

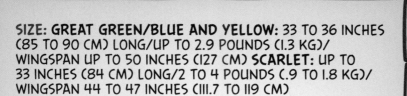

**SIZE: GREAT GREEN/BLUE AND YELLOW:** 33 TO 36 INCHES (85 TO 90 CM) LONG/UP TO 2.9 POUNDS (1.3 KG)/ WINGSPAN UP TO 50 INCHES (127 CM) **SCARLET:** UP TO 33 INCHES (84 CM) LONG/2 TO 4 POUNDS (.9 TO 1.8 KG)/ WINGSPAN 44 TO 47 INCHES (111.7 TO 119 CM)

**ON THE MENU: GREAT GREEN/BLUE AND YELLOW:** FRUIT, NUTS, SEEDS, CLAY **SCARLET:** NUTS, LEAVES, BERRIES, INSECTS, SEEDS, CLAY

**FUN FACT:** MACAWS CAN EAT FRUIT WITH SEEDS THAT ARE POISONOUS TO OTHER ANIMALS. THEY ALSO GATHER ON RIVERBANKS TO EAT CLAY. SCIENTISTS THINK EATING THE CLAY SOMEHOW MAKES THOSE POISON SEEDS HARMLESS.

SO MANY COLORS!

**BLUE AND YELLOW MACAW**
Each morning, these macaws head into the sky in groups of 100 or more—an enormous, flapping cloud of blue and yellow—to search for fruit, nuts, and seeds.

**GREAT GREEN MACAW**
A macaw's beak is tough enough to crack open nuts and seeds to get at the meat inside. But there are gentler uses for those beaks, too—like cleaning tiny bugs from one another's feathers. They hang out in small family groups of five to seven.

**SCARLET MACAW**
Macaws are fast fliers and can zip along at 35 miles an hour (56 km/h). What do they have to fear? Jaguars, monkeys, snakes, toucans, humans, and faster-flying harpy eagles.

# BLUE MORPHO BUTTERFLY

HE'S BROWN.

When a blue morpho's wings are closed, it is perfectly camouflaged. But when this butterfly opens those dull brown wings, wow! The color is almost too blue to be real. When it flies away, flashing brown-blue in the sunlight, it seems to appear and disappear right before your eyes.

NO, HE ISN'T. HE'S BLUE.

Blue morphos are some of the largest butterflies in the world. Like all butterflies, they suck juice from rotting fruit through a thin, strawlike tube called a proboscis.

YOU'RE BOTH RIGHT. HE'S BROWN-BLUE.

WINGSPAN: 5 TO 8 INCHES (13 TO 20 CM)

ON THE MENU: CATERPILLAR STAGE: LEAVES BUTTERFLY STAGE: JUICE OF ROTTED FRUIT

FUN FACT: PILOTS FLYING OVER THE RAIN FOREST SOMETIMES LOOK DOWN TO SEE MASSES OF BLUE MORPHOS RESTING IN THE TREETOPS.

# BUTTERFLIES OF THE AMAZON

**EMERGENT**

The rain forest is home to butterflies of every color imaginable. Some like to stay close to the ground, while others flutter through canopy branches or flit above the tallest emergent trees. Some gather by the hundreds. Others spend most of their time alone.

LOOK, THAT ONE HAS A TATTOO!

**WINGSPANS: TIGER LONGWING:** 1.65 TO 2 INCHES (4 TO 5 CM) **CRAMER'S 88:** 1.2 TO 1.6 INCHES (3 TO 4 CM) **BLUSHING PHANTOM:** 1.65 TO 2 INCHES (4 TO 5 CM) **OWL BUTTERFLY:** 5.5 TO 6.25 INCHES (14 TO 16 CM)

**ON THE MENU:** ROTTING FRUIT

**FUN FACT:** SOME PEOPLE LIVING IN THE AMAZON BELIEVE THAT FINDING A CRAMER'S 88 BUTTERFLY IN THEIR HOME WILL BRING THEM GOOD LUCK.

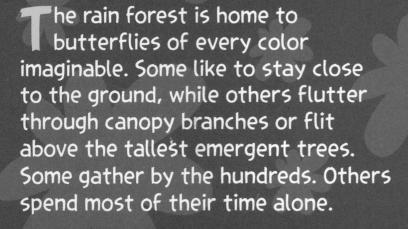

**TIGER LONGWING**
Longwings spend their nights in large groups, hanging on a single tree branch, packed tightly together. They'll return to the same branch night after night.

## BLUSHING PHANTOM
These little butterflies flit along the forest floor, rarely stopping for more than a few seconds. Their clear wings look like they've been dipped in pink paint.

## OWL BUTTERFLY
Owl butterflies are most active around sunset, when there are fewer lizards out looking for a meal. When they are caterpillars (before becoming butterflies), they love to eat the leaves of banana plants. Growers consider them pests.

## CRAMER'S 88
Hmm. Guess how these butterflies got their name? Yep, the pattern on their wings looks like the number 88. Some types of this butterfly sport 89s instead.

I CAN'T WAIT TO EXPLORE OUR RAIN FOREST. WE'LL HAVE TO DO OUR BEST TO PROTECT IT!

RIGHT, RED. WE'LL ALL DO OUR PARTS. NOW LET'S CLEAN UP!

CA-CAW!

ONCE THE BIRDS FINISHED CLEANING UP THE MESS THE PIGGIES MADE, THEY BEGAN EXPLORING THEIR OWN RAIN FOREST TO SEE WHAT COOL NEW FRIENDS LIVE THERE.

117

# QUIZ TIME!

**I.** Many animals that hunt at night have large eyes. Which of these animals do you think are night hunters?

**a.** margay      **b.** Amazon horned frog      **c.** giant anteater      **d.** potoo

a

b

c

d

**2.** Five Brazilian tapirs went for a walk. Two decided to turn back. How many were left?
5 - 2 = ?

**3.** Match these feet with the rain forest animal to which they belong.

     glass frog          jaguar          scarlet ibis

a

b

c

118

## 4. Which two foods might a hungry lizard choose?

a

b

c

## 5. These animals lost their tails! Can you match them up?

jaguar

iguana

coatimundi

macaw

a

b

c

d

**6.** Uh-oh! This little black-handed spider monkey is lost. With your finger, trace the path that will take him home.

**7.** Below are scrambled rain forest words. Can you unscramble them?

a. oAnzam     b. mwaac     c. lcakb anicam     d. raycabap

**8.** Some letters are missing from these animals' names. Can you fill in the blanks?

a. hoa_zin    b. _aguar    c. tou_an    d. ki_kajou

**9.** Starting with the smallest, can you count these monkeys from smallest to largest?

**10.** Which three animals belong in the same group? How are they alike?

a. toucan    b. jaguar    c. harpy eagle    d. scarlet ibis    e. anaconda

# BONUS ACTIVITIES

## Grow a miniature rain forest
### (gardening)

Leaf-cutter ants are the gardeners of the rain forest. Start your own flowers, herbs, or vegetables in early spring. You'll need potting soil, an envelope of seeds, and a biodegradable egg carton. Fill each well with potting soil. Press a seed (or more than one, depending on package directions) into the soil with your finger, and cover it with dirt. Place it in a sunny window, water regularly, and watch seedlings reach for the sun. When the weather warms, you can plant the entire carton outdoors (or cut it into smaller sections and plant in containers) and watch your seedlings grow.

## Howler map
### (mapping)

Howler monkeys stick to their own neighborhood. Draw a map of your neighborhood. Include houses, streets and sidewalks, big trees, mailboxes, large buildings, parks, etc. Who else lives in your neighborhood besides your own family?

## Lizard tag
### (game)

Some lizards hunt by chasing insects. Gather a few friends in a large area where everyone can crawl around on their hands and knees. One person is the hungry lizard, and everyone else is an insect. The lizard tries to capture (tag) a scurrying insect for its dinner. When an insect is caught, it becomes the next lizard.

## Build a burrow
### (imagination)

Goliath bird-eating spiders spend their days in underground burrows. Make your own burrow by draping blankets over a small table or a few chairs (turned backside-in). Spiders don't need flashlights or pillows, but you'll probably want those so you can stay in your burrow and read a stack of good books.

## Backyard bugs
### (observation)

In one hour, how many different kinds of insects can you find in your own backyard? Make a list. Look for ants, beetles, butterflies, centipedes, and flies. What others can you find?

## Monkey match
### (matching)

There are so many monkeys living in the Amazon! To become better at telling them apart, create a matching game to play. First, look at the six kinds of monkeys in this book. Then draw and color just their faces on index cards, two of each kind (writing the monkey's name below its face). Look for ways each monkey looks different from the others. Draw the golden lion tamarin with an orange mane of hair around its face, for example. The capuchin has a heart-shaped pink face surrounded by white fur. The noisy howler could be shown with its mouth open wide, etc. When your cards are finished, lay them facedown and try to match sets.

## Use your pincers
### (dexterity)

Hercules beetles have strong pincers they use to move obstacles many times their own weight. What can you lift by pinching together your pointer finger and middle finger? Can you lift a pencil? A spoon? A chair?

## Food or not?
### (deduction)

Golden lion tamarins feel into holes and cracks for the insects they like to eat. Would your fingers recognize food you couldn't see? Have an adult put a number of small items into a paper bag. Some should be bits of dry food (cereal, gummies, fish-shaped crackers, etc.) and others should be things you wouldn't eat (paper clips, an eraser, a penny, etc.). Put a hand into the bag and feel around. Using only your fingers, can you work out which items are food and which are not?

## Measure your wingspan
### (measuring)

When king vultures fly, the distance across their open wings (wingspan) is 5 feet (1.5 m). Spread your arms as wide as possible. Have an adult use a tape measure or yardstick to measure your fingertip-to-fingertip "wingspan." Do you think this number was the same last year? Do you think it will be the same next year? Measure somebody else's wingspan. Is theirs wider or narrower than your own?

## Make up a story
### (storytelling)

Little monkeys like to explore with their friends. Make up a story about a young monkey who runs into trouble while exploring. What if he saw a jaguar or became lost? How would he get out of trouble?

## Perfect patterns
### (art)

Anacondas have patterns of spots and swirls on their snaky skin. Draw an anaconda and color your own design on its skin. Use spots or squares or triangles or any shapes you wish to create a repeating pattern such as spot, spot, square, spot, spot, square.

## Camo pants
### (deduction)

Baby tapirs have camouflaging back stripes that help hide them from predators above. Go through this book and point out which animals use camouflage and which do not. Discuss why it's fine for some animals to be brightly colored and why others must blend into their surroundings.

## Make a butterfly
### (craft)

Many Amazon butterflies are bright and colorful. With a white paper coffee filter and pipe cleaner, you can create a butterfly of your own design. First, flatten the coffee filter on a newspaper or paper towel. With two or three colored markers, scribble lines and shapes on the filters. Dip a paintbrush into a small bowl of water and splatter drops onto your coffee filters. (A water-filled spray bottle may be used instead. Either way, use as little water as possible to keep from diluting colors.) Watch the colors slowly blend together. Let the filter dry completely. Now, scrunch the filter into a bow tie shape and wrap a pipe cleaner to hold it in place, leaving the ends long enough to become curled antennae. A butterfly!

## Call of the wild
### (communication)

Squirrel monkeys use 26 different calls to communicate with one another. Without using words, what kind of monkey call would you make to let others know: a) you're lost, b) you're hungry, c) you're angry, d) you want to play.

## Wait & watch
### (concentration)

Great potoos and harpy eagles can sit for hours without moving as they wait and watch for prey to appear. Sit in a chair near a clock with a minute hand. Except for breathing and blinking, how many seconds (or minutes) can you sit without moving? Try it with a friend, and see who can be still the longest.

## Thumb wrestling
### (dexterity)

Toucans like a friendly game of beak wrestling. Try thumb wrestling with a friend. Facing one another, both of you should curl the fingers of your right hands and link your fingers together, thumbs up. Now, try to catch and hold down the other player's thumb for three seconds.

## Kinkajou moves
### (following directions)

Kinkajous can change direction easily because of the way their ankles are made. Stand in the middle of a room. Take one step in whatever direction someone calls. "Right!" "Left!" "Forward!" "Back!" Orders should get faster and faster, until you make a mistake. Then take your turn being the caller.

## Snake slither
### (exercise)

Anacondas have a tough time dragging their heavy bodies around on the ground. What if you had to move like a snake? Without using your hands or legs, can you move around the room? Hint: Try rocking your body side to side.

## Colorful iguanas
### (art)

Green iguanas come in many colors. Their skin is smooth or bumpy. Looking at this book's iguana page, draw an iguana on another sheet of paper. Color its head red. Color its body blue. Color its tail brown and its feet green.

## Spiderwebs
### (craft)

Rain forest spiders spin many types of webs. You can make one of your own to hang in your room. Here's how: Cut the center out of a foam plate. Use a hole punch to make holes around the plate's rim. Cut a six to eight foot (1.8 to 2.4 m) length of string or yarn. Poke an end through one of the holes. Tape it to the back of the plate so it doesn't come loose. Now poke the other end of the yarn through a hole on the other side of the plate. Keep weaving the yarn back and forth through the holes to create a web. Tape the last bit of yarn to the back of the plate, and cut off any leftover yarn. If you want to hang your web, cut another short length of yarn and thread it through two close-together holes at the top of the plate. Tape securely. If you'd like, slip a plastic spider ring somewhere on your web.

# GLOSSARY

**BASIN**
A large area of land whose water is drained by a river and its tributaries

**CAMOUFLAGE**
The colors and patterns of an animal's skin or fur that help it blend into its surroundings

**CLIMATE**
What the weather is like over long periods of time

**COLONY**
A large group of related insects living together

**DECOMPOSE**
Rot and fall apart

**ECHOLOCATION**
Locating objects by reflected sound

**NECTAR**
Sugary fluid made by plants

**NUTRIENT**
Something that helps animals grow and live

**OMNIVORE**
An animal that will eat both animals and plants

**PINCERS**
Claws that pinch together

**POISONOUS**
Producing a substance that can cause sickness or death

**PREDATOR**
An animal that hunts others for food

**PREY**
An animal that is hunted by another for food

**SAPLING**
A small, growing tree

**SIDE-NECKED**
A type of turtle that cannot pull its neck straight back into its shell, but only bend it sideways

**TERRITORY**
The area an animal considers its home

**TRIBUTARIES**
Smaller rivers and streams that flow into a bigger one

**WINGSPAN**
Measurement across outspread wings, from tip to tip

# INDEX

**Boldface** indicates illustrations.

INDEX

# PHOTO CREDITS

**Published by the National Geographic Society**
John M. Fahey, Chairman of the Board and Chief Executive Officer
Declan Moore, Executive Vice President; President, Publishing and Travel
Melina Gerosa Bellows, Publisher; Chief Creative Officer, Books, Kids, and Family

**Prepared by the Book Division**
Hector Sierra, Senior Vice President and General Manager
Nancy Laties Feresten, Senior Vice President, Kids Publishing and Media
Jennifer Emmett, Vice President, Editorial Director, Kids Books
Eva Absher-Schantz, Design Director, Kids Publishing and Media
Jay Sumner, Director of Photography, Kids Publishing
R. Gary Colbert, Production Director
Jennifer A. Thornton, Director of Managing Editorial

**Staff for This Book**
Becky Baines, Editor
Amy Briggs, Project Editor
Lori Epstein, Senior Photo Editor
Annette Kiesow, Photo Editor
Dawn Ripple McFadin, Designer
Ariane Szu-Tu, Editorial Assistant
Callie Broaddus, Design Production Assistant
Margaret Leist, Photo Assistant
Carl Mehler, Director of Maps
Stuart Armstrong, Map Art
Grace Hill, Associate Managing Editor
Michael O'Connor, Production Editor
Lewis R. Bassford, Production Manager
Susan Borke, Legal and Business Affairs

**Rovio Entertainment Ltd.**
Sanna Lukander, Vice President of Book Publishing
Anna Makkonen, Graphic Designer
Mari Elomäki, Project Editor
Nita Ukkonen, Project Editor

**Production Services**
Phillip L. Schlosser, Senior Vice President
Chris Brown, Vice President, NG Book Manufacturing
George Bounelis, Senior Production Manager
Nicole Elliott, Director of Production
Rachel Faulise, Manager
Robert L. Barr, Manager